TOP 12

TAX DEDUCTIONS

YOU MIGHT HAVE MISSED

**Tax Tips For People Who Do Their
Own Federal Taxes**

TAXASSURANCES, LLC.

Printed in the United States of America

First Printing, 2017

ISBN-13: 978-1540656728

ISBN-10: 1540656721

Table of Contents

Introduction

Every year, our tax clients ask what other tax benefits they can take advantage of. And with every client, that answer is different and depends on their individual circumstances.

But even though every client has a different set of circumstances, some tax benefits are standard and basic under the IRS tax code. And people may not be aware of them. Why?

Because the IRS tax code is long and complicated. Even some of what we have in this book is somewhat detailed. There are a lot of situations for the IRS to consider. But most people don't have the time, interest or energy to go through it all. That's our job here at TaxAssurances, LLC.

This book highlights some basic benefits available to taxpayers they may not be aware of. And most importantly, we provide exact IRS wording on what they want in specific situations.

We do offer this word of caution. For those individuals that aren't sure if they have a simple or complicated tax return, we strongly recommend that they seek professional, personalized tax help. TaxAssurances and other firms are here for that. The savings and clarity are worth it.

Also, because of specific personal circumstances, readers should not solely rely on this book for guidance.

We put this Top 12 list together for people who file simple tax returns. Nothing complicated or complex. It's designed to complement them as they prepare their own tax returns.

They've gone to the store and bought the prep software for $30 or $40 and are comfortable doing their own returns.

Also, they don't want to pay a tax preparer a bunch of money for a simple return. And the last thing they want to do is sit in an office waiting for the preparer to finish the return. They want this process to be quick and easy.

These tax filers do understand however that there might be simple and easy tax benefits that they can take advantage of that they might not be aware of. This book helps them out.

This book does not cover itemized deductions or handling homeownership. It also doesn't cover having investments or rental properties.

The layout and chapters are simple. They match up with the tax benefits themselves. So if a reader wants a quick overview, they can just go through the table of contents. There they can find the benefit that may apply to their life and go to that chapter.

So hopefully this book provides just what readers are looking for in tax benefits for their life.

Chapter 1 Child Tax Credit

Besides being a blessing to a parent's life, children can provide some real tax benefits. There are a few to consider.

First and foremost, they increase the number of exemptions and deductions a parent can have on their tax return. That's a great start. But in this chapter, we'll specifically discuss the child tax credit.

The $1,000 credit per child helps lower a parent's tax liability for the year. And parents can use the credit for each one of their children.

There are some requirements to take the child tax credit and the IRS has provided some guidance. Here's exactly what they say:

A qualifying child for purposes of the child tax credit is a child who:

1. Is your son, daughter, stepchild, foster child, adopted child, brother, sister, stepbrother, stepsister, half-brother, half-sister, or a descendant of any of them (for example, your grandchild, niece, or nephew),

2. Will be under age 17 at the end of the year,

3. Did not provide over half of his or her own support for the year,

4. Lived with you for more than half of the year (with certain exceptions),

5. Is claimed as a dependent on your return,

6. Does not file a joint return for the year (or files it only to claim a refund of withheld income tax or estimated tax paid), and

7. Was a U.S. citizen, a U.S. national, or a U.S. resident alien. For more information, see Pub. 519, U.S. Tax Guide for Aliens. If the child was adopted, see Adopted child.

Now, it is worth noting that the IRS imposes limits on taking the credit. Also, some parents may not be able to take the credit at all. Here's what they says about those limits specifically:

You must reduce the maximum credit amount of $1,000 for each child if either (1) or (2) applies.

1. The amount on Form 1040, line 47; Form 1040A, line 30; or Form 1040NR, line 45, is less than the credit. If this amount is zero, you cannot take this credit because there is no any tax to reduce. But you may be able to take the additional child tax credit. This credit is for certain individuals who get less than the full amount of the child tax credit. The additional child tax credit may give you a refund even if you do not owe any tax.

2. Your modified adjusted gross income (AGI) is more than the amount shown below for your filing status.

a. Married filing jointly – $110,000.

b. Single, head of household, or qualifying widow(er) – $75,000.

c. Married filing separately – $55,000.

Now if that seems confusing don't worry. The tax prep software works out the details for you. Just know that it is a credit that should appear on your tax return if you qualify.

So if you're a parent that meets all of these qualifications, make sure you include all your child's information on your tax return. It can help lower your taxes and potentially get you a larger tax refund.

For more information about the child tax credit and the additional child tax credit, read IRS Publication 972 on the IRS.gov website.

Chapter 2 Student Loan Interest Deduction

Student loan interest that people pay during the year may be tax deductible. And that deduction may be as much as $2,500. But like anything with the IRS, it depends on the circumstances.

Here's who the IRS says can claim the student loan interest deduction:

"You can claim the deduction if all of the following apply:

- *You paid interest on a qualified student loan in the tax year.*

- *You are legally obligated to pay interest on a qualified student loan.*

- *Your filing status is not married filing separately.*

- *Your MAGI is less than a specified amount which is set annually, and*

- *You or your spouse, if filing jointly, cannot be claimed as dependents on someone else's return."*

So if you meet these requirements, make sure you get the necessary information together to take the deduction.

But where do you get the information from? The quick and easy answer is, the lender. At the end of the year, they'll send a statement with all the necessary specifics.

Below is a sample of what a year end student loan interest statement looks like. The most important box is the #1 box titled, "Student loan interest received by lender." It has the total amount of student loan interest that was paid for the year.

		CORRECTED (if checked)		
RECIPIENT'S/LENDER'S name, street address, city or town, state or province, country, ZIP or foreign postal code, and telephone number			OMB No. 1545-1576	
			2016	Student Loan Interest Statement
			Form **1098-E**	
RECIPIENT'S federal identification no.	BORROWER'S social security number	1 Student loan interest received by lender		**Copy B** **For Borrower**
BORROWER'S name and address				This is important tax information and is being furnished to the Internal Revenue Service. If you are required to file a return, a negligence penalty or other sanction may be imposed on you if the IRS determines that an underpayment of tax results because you overstated a deduction for student loan interest.
Account number (see instructions)		2 If checked, box 1 does not include loan origination fees and/or capitalized interest for loans made before September 1, 2004		

Form **1098-E** (keep for your records) www.irs.gov/form1098e Department of the Treasury - Internal Revenue Service

Now like we noted earlier, not everyone can deduct student loan interest for the year. For example, people that make over $80,000 a year and file single or head of household and $160,000 a year and file married filing jointly, cannot take the deduction. Also, those who file married filing separately cannot take the deduction at all.

There is also a gradual reduction in the amount that people can deduct leading up to the maximum income limits. Here's what the IRS says about it:

"The amount of your student loan interest deduction is phased out (gradually reduced) if your MAGI is between $65,000 and $80,000 ($130,000 and $160,000 if you file a joint return). You can't claim a student loan interest deduction if your MAGI is $80,000 or more ($160,000 or more if you file a joint return)."

So if a taxpayer's income is within this specific range, they (more likely the tax prep software) have to make adjustments to figure out the correct amount to deduct.

Here's the IRS formula for figuring out the right amount:

"If your MAGI is within the range of incomes where the credit must be reduced, you must figure your reduced deduction. To figure the phase-out, multiply your interest

5

deduction (before the phase-out, but not more than $2,500) by a fraction. The numerator (top part) is your MAGI minus $65,000 ($130,000 in the case of a joint return). The denominator (bottom part) is $15,000 ($30,000 in the case of a joint return). Subtract the result from your deduction (before the phase-out) to give you the amount you can deduct."

Bottom line, individuals that pay student loan interest during the year need to make sure they get their year-end statements from their lender. The interest they paid may be tax deductible.

For more information about the student loan interest deduction, read Publication 970 and IRS Topic 456 on the IRS.gov website.

Chapter 3 Alimony

Divorces and separations can be difficult. They mark the end of relationships that started off with so much hope, love, and passion. And anytime someone goes through a divorce there can be positive and negative effects. For example, the payment of alimony can be both positive and negative. Strange to say.

But here's what we mean. Writing the check or having money come out of an account every month to pay alimony can be a huge pain in the neck. However, the IRS gives the payer a tax deduction.

Here's how they describe what is tax deductible when it comes to divorce or separation:

"Amounts paid under divorce or separate maintenance decrees or written separation agreements entered into between you and your spouse or former spouse are considered alimony for federal tax purposes if:

- *You and your spouse or former spouse do not file a joint return with each other*

- *You pay in cash (including checks or money orders)*

- *The payment is received by (or on behalf of) your spouse or former spouse*

- *The divorce or separate maintenance decree or written separation agreement does not say the payment is not alimony*

- *If legally separated under a decree of divorce or separate maintenance, you and your former spouse are not members of the same household when you make the payment*

- *You have no liability to make the payment (in cash or property) after the death of your spouse or former spouse, and*

- *Your payment is not treated as child support or a property settlement*

It is worth noting that not all payments are considered alimony and are not tax deductible. Here's what the IRS says about that:

"Alimony does not include:

- *Child support*

- *Noncash property settlements*

- *Payments that are your spouse's part of community property income*

- *Payments to keep up the payer's property, or*

- *Use of the payer's property*

Child support is never deductible. If your decree of divorce or separate maintenance provides for alimony and child support, and you pay less than the total required, the payments apply first to child support. Any remaining amount is considered alimony.

Noncash property settlements, whether in a lump sum or installments, do not qualify as alimony.

Voluntary payments (that is, payments not required by a divorce decree or separation instrument) do not qualify as alimony."

So as you can see, for taxpayers that are going through a divorce and have to pay alimony there is a silver lining. The payments are tax deductible.

For more information about the alimony tax deduction, read IRS Topic 452 on the IRS.gov website.

Chapter 4   Education Expenses

Paying for an education past high school may be tax deductible. Also, paying for someone else to go to school after graduating from high school may be tax deductible.

It goes without saying that getting more education likely helps a person's chances in life. It also likely helps the people around them.

Because of that, the government wants to encourage individuals to learn more. That's why the potential for a tax deduction goes up to $4,000.

Here's who the IRS says can claim the education expense deduction:

Qualified education expenses must be paid by:

- *You or your spouse if you file a joint return,*

- *A student you claim as a dependent on your return, or*

- *A third party including relatives or friends.*

Here's who the IRS says CANNOT claim the education expense deduction:

"You cannot claim an education credit when:

- *Someone else, such as your parents, list you as a dependent on their tax return*

- *Your filing status is married filing separately*

- *You already claimed or deducted another higher education benefit using the same student or same expenses (see Education Benefits: No Double Benefits Allowed for more information)*

- *You (or your spouse) were a nonresident alien for any part of the year and did not choose to be treated as a resident alien for tax purposes (find more information in Publication 519, U.S. Tax Guide for Aliens)"*

Now there are a few ways to take the education expense deduction and taxpayers (with their software) will be able to decide which is best. But here is what the IRS says about which benefit they can use:

"You can choose the education benefit that will give you the lowest tax."

The first type of education expense deduction is called the Tuition and Fees deduction. This deduction has a maximum benefit of $4,000 for the year.

Below is the IRS form used (by the software) to figure out the amount of the Tuition and Fees deduction.

Form **8917**		Tuition and Fees Deduction		OMB No. 1645-0074
Department of the Treasury Internal Revenue Service		▶ Attach to Form 1040 or Form 1040A. ▶ Information about Form 8917 and its instructions is at *www.irs.gov/form8917*.		**2015** Attachment Sequence No. **60**

Name(s) shown on return: Tim Pfister

Your social security number: 000-00-5432

⚠ **CAUTION** You **cannot** take both an education credit from Form 8863 and the tuition and fees deduction from this form for the same student for the same tax year.

Before you begin: ✔ To see if you qualify for this deduction, see *Who Can Take the Deduction* in the instructions below.

✔ If you file Form 1040, figure any write-in adjustments to be entered on the dotted line next to Form 1040, line 36. See the 2015 Form 1040 instructions for line 36.

1	(a) Student's name (as shown on page 1 of your tax return)		(b) Student's social security number (as shown on page 1 of your tax return)	(c) Adjusted qualified expenses (see instructions)
	First name	Last name		
	Tim	Pfister	000-00-5432	3,800

2	Add the amounts on line 1, column (c), and enter the total	**2**	3,800

3	Enter the amount from Form 1040, line 22, or Form 1040A, line 15	**3**	20,000

4 Enter the total from either:

• Form 1040, lines 23 through 33, plus any write-in adjustments entered on the dotted line next to Form 1040, line 36, **or**

• Form 1040A, lines 16 through 18.	**4**	-0-

5	Subtract line 4 from line 3.* If the result is more than $80,000 ($160,000 if married filing jointly), **stop**; you cannot take the deduction for tuition and fees	**5**	20,000

*If you are filing Form 2555, 2555-EZ, or 4563, or you are excluding income from Puerto Rico, see *Effect of the Amount of Your Income on the Amount of Your Deduction* in Pub. 970, chapter 6, to figure the amount to enter on line 5.

6 **Tuition and fees deduction.** Is the amount on line 5 more than $65,000 ($130,000 if married filing jointly)?

☐ **Yes.** Enter the smaller of line 2, or $2,000. ⎫

☐ **No.** Enter the smaller of line 2, or $4,000. ⎰ . . . . | **6** | 3,800

Also enter this amount on Form 1040, line 34, or Form 1040A, line 19.

For Paperwork Reduction Act Notice, see your tax return instructions.   Cat. No. 37728P   Form **8917** (2015)

As stated throughout this book, there are restrictions on who can take certain deductions. The Tuition and Fees deductions are no different. Here's who the IRS says cannot take advantage of the tuition and fees deduction:

"You can't claim the tuition and fees deduction if any of the following apply.

- *Your filing status is married filing separately.*

- *Another person can claim an exemption for you as a dependent on his or her tax return. You can't take the deduction even if the other person doesn't actually claim that exemption.*

- *Your modified adjusted gross income (MAGI) is more than $80,000 ($160,000 if filing a joint return).*

- *You (or your spouse) were a nonresident alien for any part of 2015 and the nonresident alien didn't elect to be treated as a resident alien for tax purposes. More information on nonresident aliens can be found in Pub. 519."*

There is also a reduction in the deductible amount someone can take based on their income. To describe it in a nutshell, the more money someone makes, the less chance they have of taking the tuition and fees deduction.

Here's how the IRS describes it:

"If your MAGI isn't more than $65,000 ($130,000 if you are married filing jointly), your maximum tuition and fees deduction is $4,000. If your MAGI is larger than $65,000 ($130,000 if you are married filing jointly) but isn't more than $80,000 ($160,000 if you are married filing jointly), your maximum deduction is $2,000. No tuition and fees deduction is allowed if your MAGI is larger than $80,000 ($160,000 if you are married filing jointly)"

Another way individuals can take a deduction for going to school is through Education Credits. And there are two types.

One type of credit is called the American Opportunities Tax Credit and the other is called the Lifetime Learning Credit.

The American Opportunity Tax Credit has a maximum annual benefit of $2,500. Here's who the IRS says qualifies for the American Opportunities Tax Credit:

"To be eligible for AOTC, the student must:

- ❖ *Be pursuing a degree or other recognized education credential*
- ❖ *Be enrolled at least half-time for at least one academic period* beginning in the tax year*
- ❖ *Not have finished the first four years of higher education at the beginning of the tax year*
- ❖ *Not have claimed the AOTC or the former Hope credit for more than four tax years*
- ❖ *Not have a felony drug conviction at the end of the tax year*

*Academic Period can be semesters, trimesters, quarters or any other period of study such as a summer school session. The schools determine the academic periods. For schools that use clock or credit hours and do not have academic terms, the payment period may be treated as an academic period."

Here is the form to figure out how much of a credit an individual can have using the American Opportunities Credit:

Form **8863**	**Education Credits** **(American Opportunity and Lifetime Learning Credits)**	OMB No. 1545-0074
Department of the Treasury Internal Revenue Service (99)	▶ Attach to Form 1040 or Form 1040A. ▶ Information about Form 8863 and its separate instructions is at *www.irs.gov/form8863*.	20**15** Attachment Sequence No. **50**

Name(s) shown on return: Dave and Valerie Jones

Your social security number: 001 00 0000

> **CAUTION** Complete a separate Part III on page 2 for each student for whom you are claiming either credit before you complete Parts I and II.

Part I   Refundable American Opportunity Credit

1	After completing Part III for each student, enter the total of all amounts from all Parts III, line 30	**1**	2,500
2	Enter: $180,000 if married filing jointly; $90,000 if single, head of household, or qualifying widow(er) **2** 180,000		
3	Enter the amount from Form 1040, line 38, or Form 1040A, line 22. If you are filing Form 2555, 2555-EZ, or 4563, or you are excluding income from Puerto Rico, see Pub. 970 for the amount to enter **3** 120,000		
4	Subtract line 3 from line 2. If zero or less, **stop**; you cannot take any education credit **4** 60,000		
5	Enter: $20,000 if married filing jointly; $10,000 if single, head of household, or qualifying widow(er) **5** 20,000		
6	If line 4 is: • Equal to or more than line 5, enter 1.000 on line 6 • Less than line 5, divide line 4 by line 5. Enter the result as a decimal (rounded to at least three places)	**6**	1. 000
7	Multiply line 1 by line 6. **Caution:** If you were under age 24 at the end of the year **and** meet the conditions described in the instructions, you **cannot** take the refundable American opportunity credit; skip line 8, enter the amount from line 7 on line 9, and check this box ▶ ☐	**7**	2,500
8	**Refundable American opportunity credit.** Multiply line 7 by 40% (.40). Enter the amount here and on Form 1040, line 68, or Form 1040A, line 44. Then go to line 9 below.	**8**	1,000

Part II   Nonrefundable Education Credits

9	Subtract line 8 from line 7. Enter here and on line 2 of the Credit Limit Worksheet (see instructions)	**9**	1,500
10	After completing Part III for each student, enter the total of all amounts from all Parts III, line 31. If zero, skip lines 11 through 17, enter -0- on line 18, and go to line 19	**10**	7,000
11	Enter the smaller of line 10 or $10,000	**11**	7,000
12	Multiply line 11 by 20% (.20)	**12**	1,400
13	Enter: $130,000 if married filing jointly; $65,000 if single, head of household, or qualifying widow(er) **13** 130,000		
14	Enter the amount from Form 1040, line 38, or Form 1040A, line 22. If you are filing Form 2555, 2555-EZ, or 4563, or you are excluding income from Puerto Rico, see Pub. 970 for the amount to enter **14** 120,000		
15	Subtract line 14 from line 13. If zero or less, skip lines 16 and 17, enter -0- on line 18, and go to line 19 **15** 10,000		
16	Enter: $20,000 if married filing jointly; $10,000 if single, head of household, or qualifying widow(er) **16** 20,000		
17	If line 15 is: • Equal to or more than line 16, enter 1.000 on line 17 and go to line 18 • Less than line 16, divide line 15 by line 16. Enter the result as a decimal (rounded to at least three places)	**17**	. 500
18	Multiply line 12 by line 17. Enter here and on line 1 of the Credit Limit Worksheet (see instructions) ▶	**18**	700
19	**Nonrefundable education credits.** Enter the amount from line 7 of the Credit Limit Worksheet (see instructions) here and on Form 1040, line 50, or Form 1040A, line 33	**19**	1,003

For Paperwork Reduction Act Notice, see your tax return instructions.   Cat. No. 25379M   Form **8863** (2015)

The Lifetime Learning Credit has a maximum benefit for the year of $2,000. And here's who the IRS says qualifies for it:

To claim an LLC, you must meet all three of the following:

- *You, your dependent or a third party pay qualified education expenses for higher education*

- *You, your dependent or a third party pay the education expenses for an eligible student enrolled at an eligible educational institution*
- *The eligible student is yourself, your spouse or a dependent you listed on your tax return*

And like the American Opportunities Tax Credit, here is the form to figure out how much of a credit someone can take for the year:

Form **8863**	**Education Credits** (American Opportunity and Lifetime Learning Credits)	OMB No. 1545-0074
Department of the Treasury Internal Revenue Service (99)	▶ Attach to Form 1040 or Form 1040A. ▶ Information about Form 8863 and its separate instructions is at *www.irs.gov/form8863*.	2015 Attachment Sequence No. **50**

Name(s) shown on return: Dave and Valerie Jones

Your social security number: 001 00 0000

⚠ **CAUTION** Complete a separate Part III on page 2 for each student for whom you are claiming either credit before you complete Parts I and II.

Part I	**Refundable American Opportunity Credit**		
1	After completing Part III for each student, enter the total of all amounts from all Parts III, line 30	**1**	2,500
2	Enter: $180,000 if married filing jointly; $90,000 if single, head of household, or qualifying widow(er)	**2** 180,000	
3	Enter the amount from Form 1040, line 38, or Form 1040A, line 22. If you are filing Form 2555, 2555-EZ, or 4563, or you are excluding income from Puerto Rico, see Pub. 970 for the amount to enter	**3** 120,000	
4	Subtract line 3 from line 2. If zero or less, **stop**; you cannot take any education credit	**4** 60,000	
5	Enter: $20,000 if married filing jointly; $10,000 if single, head of household, or qualifying widow(er)	**5** 20,000	
6	If line 4 is: • Equal to or more than line 5, enter 1.000 on line 6 • Less than line 5, divide line 4 by line 5. Enter the result as a decimal (rounded to at least three places)	**6**	1.000
7	Multiply line 1 by line 6. **Caution:** If you were under age 24 at the end of the year and meet the conditions described in the instructions, you **cannot** take the refundable American opportunity credit; skip line 8, enter the amount from line 7 on line 9, and check this box ▶ ☐	**7**	2,500
8	**Refundable American opportunity credit.** Multiply line 7 by 40% (.40). Enter the amount here and on Form 1040, line 68, or Form 1040A, line 44. Then go to line 9 below.	**8**	1,000
Part II	**Nonrefundable Education Credits**		
9	Subtract line 8 from line 7. Enter here and on line 2 of the Credit Limit Worksheet (see instructions)	**9**	1,500
10	After completing Part III for each student, enter the total of all amounts from all Parts III, line 31. If zero, skip lines 11 through 17, enter -0- on line 18, and go to line 19	**10**	7,000
11	Enter the smaller of line 10 or $10,000	**11**	7,000
12	Multiply line 11 by 20% (.20)	**12**	1,400
13	Enter: $130,000 if married filing jointly; $65,000 if single, head of household, or qualifying widow(er)	**13** 130,000	
14	Enter the amount from Form 1040, line 38, or Form 1040A, line 22. If you are filing Form 2555, 2555-EZ, or 4563, or you are excluding income from Puerto Rico, see Pub. 970 for the amount to enter	**14** 120,000	
15	Subtract line 14 from line 13. If zero or less, skip lines 16 and 17, enter -0- on line 18, and go to line 19	**15** 10,000	
16	Enter: $20,000 if married filing jointly; $10,000 if single, head of household, or qualifying widow(er)	**16** 20,000	
17	If line 15 is: • Equal to or more than line 16, enter 1.000 on line 17 and go to line 18 • Less than line 16, divide line 15 by line 16. Enter the result as a decimal (rounded to at least three places)	**17**	.500
18	Multiply line 12 by line 17. Enter here and on line 1 of the Credit Limit Worksheet (see instructions) ▶	**18**	700
19	**Nonrefundable education credits.** Enter the amount from line 7 of the Credit Limit Worksheet (see instructions) here and on Form 1040, line 50, or Form 1040A, line 33	**19**	1,003

For Paperwork Reduction Act Notice, see your tax return instructions.   Cat. No. 25379M   Form **8863** (2015)

Again, there are three ways to use the cost of a higher education to reduce a tax bill. Ultimately, IRS rules and the tax prep software figures out which credit or deduction the taxpayers can take.

So now that we having an understanding of what types of tax benefits getting an education provides, let's examine what expenses do and do not qualify.

First and foremost, tuition expenses qualify. And not only that, they are usually the largest of all the education related expenses. According to the IRS the next list of expenses also qualify for a tax benefit.

- Books, supplies, and equipment
- Other necessary expenses

The statement below is a sample of where individuals get some of their total expenses from. Usually, it's sent by the school.

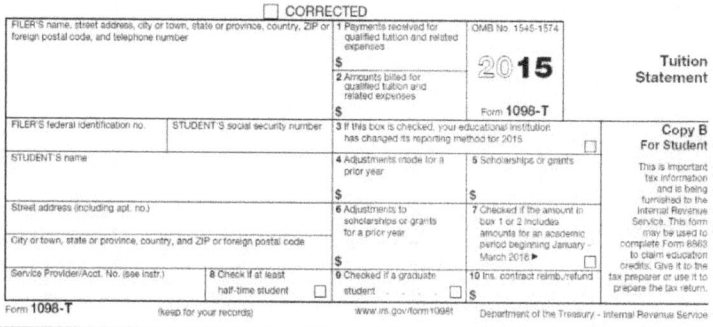

But not everything is deductible. Here are the following expenses that the IRS says CANNOT be deducted for education expenses:

"Expenses that Do Not Qualify

Even if you pay the following expenses to enroll or attend the school, the following are not qualified education expenses:

- *Room and board*

- *Insurance*

- *Medical expenses (including student health fees)*

- *Transportation*

- *Similar personal, living or family expenses*

Sports, games, hobbies or non-credit course

Expenses for sports, games, hobbies or non-credit courses do not qualify for the education credits or tuition and fees deduction, except when the course or activity is part of the student's degree program. For the Lifetime Learning Credit only, these expenses qualify if the course helps the student acquire or improve job skills."

Having gone over all of this, the IRS however does require anyone that takes an education expense deduction to make a few adjustments to the total amount deductible. They say this, *"Reduce the qualified educational expenses for each academic period by the amount of tax-free educational assistance allocable to that academic period."*

Simply put, they want taxpayers to reduce their deductions by any tax-free income they receive for the year. What does that include? This:

- Scholarships
- Fellowships
- Tax-free Grants
- Tax-free Pell Grants

- Employer-provided educational assistance
- Veteran's educational assistance

"Amounts that don't reduce qualified education expenses. Don't reduce qualified education expenses by amounts paid with funds the student receives as:

Payment for services, such as wages;

A loan;

A gift;

An inheritance; or

A withdrawal from the student's personal savings.

Don't reduce the qualified education expenses by any scholarship or fellowship grant reported as income on the student's tax return in the following situations.

The use of the money is restricted, by the terms of the scholarship or fellowship grant, to costs of attendance (such as room and board) other than qualified education expenses as defined in qualified education expenses in chapter 1.

The use of the money isn't restricted."

Now this is a lot in terms of information about education credits, but like we said earlier in this book, tax software will automatically calculate which deduction is the most beneficial.

So taxpayers that had qualifying education expenses for the year want to make sure they add them all up. That way they can make sure they take advantage of their tax benefit.

For more information about Education Credits, read IRS Publication 970 on the IRS.gov website.

Chapter 5 Business Expenses

This is the chapter that our clients find the most helpful when it comes to finding tax benefits. It's all about starting a business, running a business and keep track of business expenses.

Starting a business either full time or part time is a great way to take advantage of some tax benefits. Taking the deductions doesn't even require that the business be formally incorporated. It can be something simple. But the IRS does have guidelines on what is considered a business. Here's what they say:

"An activity qualifies as a business if your primary purpose of engaging in the activity is for income or profits and you are involved in the activity with continuity and regularity. For example, a sporadic activity or a hobby does not qualify as a business."

Once a person realizes that they have a qualified business, the search is on for tax benefits. The good news is, the IRS provides a lot in terms of deductible expenses that can help reduce someone's tax liability.

But there is one thing to keep in mind, receipts. If a person ever gets audited by the IRS they want to make sure they have a record of the expenses. Without them, the IRS may not allow the expenses and in turn increase someone's tax liability. So keep receipts.

So let's cut to the chase. Here's a list of some of the most used business expenses that can give individuals a tax benefit when they first start a business:

- Advertising
- Car & Truck Expenses
- Mileage deduction for business travel
- Commissions and fees
- Contract labor
- Depletion
- Depreciation
- Employee benefits
- Insurance (other than health)
- Legal and Professional Services
- Office expense
- Pension and profit sharing
- Rent
- Vehicle, machinery, and equipment
- Other business property
- Repairs and Maintenance
- Supplies
- Taxes & License
- Travel, meals, and entertainment
- Utilities
- Wages
- Other Expenses
- Home Office Deduction

There are more but this is a good start.

So taxpayers that may have had a small business on the side and didn't really think it qualified as one, want to add up all the expenses they had for the year. They may realize that they had more tax benefits than they thought.

For more information about allowed business expenses, check out IRS publication 535 on the IRS.gov website.

Chapter 6 Health Savings Accounts (HSAs)

The IRS wants to help people take care of their medical needs. And because of that, taxpayers can set up Health Savings Accounts or HSAs.

With them, the IRS provides tax benefits for the contributions to the account, interest earned on the money in the account and healthcare expense deductions taken from the account. Thus offering three types of tax incentives.

Here is how the IRS describes Health Savings Accounts or HSAs:

"A health savings account (HSA) is a tax-exempt trust or custodial account you set up with a qualified HSA trustee to pay or reimburse certain medical expenses you incur. You must be an eligible individual to qualify for an HSA.

No permission or authorization from the IRS is necessary to establish an HSA. You set up an HSA with a trustee. A qualified HSA trustee can be a bank, an insurance company, or anyone already approved by the IRS to be a trustee of individual retirement arrangements (IRAs) or Archer MSAs. The HSA can be established through a trustee that is different from your health plan provider."

Here's who the IRS says qualifies to participate in an HSA:

To be an eligible individual and qualify for an HSA, you must meet the following requirements.

- *You must be covered under a high deductible health plan (HDHP), described later, on the first day of the month.*

- *You have no other health coverage except what is permitted under other health coverage, later.*
- *You are not enrolled in Medicare.*
- *You cannot be claimed as a dependent on someone else's tax return.*
- *Under the last-month rule, you are considered to be an eligible individual for the entire year if you are an eligible individual on the first day of the last month of your tax year (December 1 for most taxpayers).*

If you meet these requirements, you are an eligible individual even if your spouse has non-HDHP family coverage, provided your spouse's coverage does not cover you.

If another taxpayer is entitled to claim an exemption for you, you cannot claim a deduction for an HSA contribution. This is true even if the other person does not actually claim your exemption.

Each spouse who is an eligible individual who wants an HSA must open a separate HSA. You cannot have a joint HSA.

So once a person realizes that they qualify for an HSA account the next question is, how much of a tax benefit does a HSAs offer? Here is how the IRS lays that out:

The amount you or any other person can contribute to your HSA depends on the type of HDHP coverage you have, your age, the date you become an eligible individual, and the date you cease to be an eligible individual. For the year, if you have self-only HDHP coverage, you can contribute up to $3,350. If you have family HDHP coverage you can contribute up to $6,750.

If you were, or were considered (under the last-month rule, discussed later), an eligible individual for the entire year and did not change your type of coverage, you can contribute the full amount based on your type of coverage. However, if you were not an eligible individual for the entire year or changed your coverage during the year, your contribution limit is the greater of:

The limitation shown on the Line 3 Limitation Chart and Worksheet in the Instructions for Form 8889, Health Savings Accounts (HSAs), or

The maximum annual HSA contribution based on your HDHP coverage (self-only or family) on the first day of the last month of your tax year.

That is a lot. We understand. But the important part is that taxpayers get their year-end summary of what they contributed to the account. And once they do, enter the information on IRS form 8889 which gives the details for the tax efficient accounting for the contributions and deductions from the HAS.

So where do individuals get the details of what happened in the HSA for the year? Their trustee.

Here's an example of the year end summary they'll send:

24

With this they simply fill in the necessary details and make sure the IRS form 8889 mentioned earlier is prepared.

So individuals looking for additional tax benefits should look at HSAs as a great way to not only save for medical reasons but also get great tax savings.

For more information about the Health Savings Account deduction, read IRS Publication 969 on the IRS.gov website.

Chapter 7 Marriage

Not only is a marriage a union based on love and trust it also offers tax benefits. For instance, married couples that file their taxes together have higher standard deductions and exemptions than individuals that file single, head of household or married filing separately. As a result, married couples that file jointly most likely have lower tax bills.

There are couples however that decide to file their tax returns separately. While they do have it as an option, here's how the IRS describes what they are giving up:

- *"If you choose married filing separately as your filing status, the following special rules apply. Because of these special rules, you usually pay more tax on a separate return than if you use another filing status you qualify for.*

- *Your tax rate generally is higher than on a joint return.*

- *Your exemption amount for figuring the alternative minimum tax is half that allowed on a joint return.*

- *You cannot take the credit for child and dependent care expenses in most cases, and the amount you can exclude from income under an employer's dependent care assistance program is limited to $2,500 (instead of $5,000). However, if you are legally separated or living apart from your spouse, you may be able to file a separate return and still take the credit. For more information about these expenses, the credit, and the exclusion, see chapter 32.*

- *You cannot take the earned income credit.*

- *You cannot take the exclusion or credit for adoption expenses in most cases.*

- *You cannot take the education credits (the American opportunity credit and lifetime learning credit) or the deduction for student loan interest.*

- *You cannot exclude any interest income from qualified U.S. savings bonds you used for higher education expenses.*

- *If you lived with your spouse at any time during the tax year:*

- *You cannot claim the credit for the elderly or the disabled, and*

- *You must include in income a greater percentage (up to 85%) of any social security or equivalent railroad retirement benefits you received.*

- *The following credits and deductions are reduced at income levels half those for a joint return:*

- *The child tax credit,*

- *The retirement savings contributions credit,*

- *The deduction for personal exemptions, and*
- *Itemized deductions.*

- *Your capital loss deduction limit is $1,500 (instead of $3,000 on a joint return).*

- *If your spouse itemizes deductions, you cannot claim the standard deduction. If you can claim the standard deduction, your basic standard deduction is half the amount allowed on a joint return.*

So as the list above suggests, if you're married or getting married, file your tax return together. There are some real tax benefits.

For more information about being married and filing tax returns, read "Filing Status" on the IRS.gov website.

Chapter 8 Moving

Many taxpayers don't realize that moving from one part of the country to another offers tax benefits.

But there are some requirements that need to be met to take the deduction. Here's how the IRS lays them out:

If you moved due to a change in your job or business location, or because you started a new job or business, you may be able to deduct your reasonable moving expenses but not any expenses for meals. You can deduct your moving expenses if you meet all three of the following requirements:

- *Your move closely relates to the start of work*
- *You meet the distance test*
- *You meet the time test*

Move Related to Start of Work - Your move must closely relate both in time and in place to the start of work at your new location. You can consider moving expenses incurred within one year from the date you first reported to work at the new location as closely related in time to the start of work. A move generally relates closely in place if the distance from your new home to the new job location is not more than the distance from your former home to the new job location. For exceptions to these requirements, see Publication 521, Moving Expenses.

The distance test - Your new workplace must be at least 50 miles farther from your old home than your old job location was from your old home. If you had no previous workplace, your new job location must be at least 50 miles from your old home.

The time test - If you are an employee, you must work full-time for at least 39 weeks during the first 12 months immediately following your arrival in the general area of your new job location. If you are self-employed, you must work full time for at least 39 weeks during the first 12 months and for a total of at least 78 weeks during the first 24 months immediately following your arrival in the general area of your new work location. There are exceptions to the time test in case of death, disability, and involuntary separation, among other things. See Publication 521 for these exceptions.

Here's what the IRS says is deductible in making the move.

Deductible Expenses

- Travel by car
- Storage
- Packaging, crating and transporting household goods and personal effects

On the other hand, here's what the IRS says is not deductible in making a move:

Nondeductible Expenses

- Car tags
- Driver's license
- Any part of the purchase price of the new home
- Expenses of buying or selling a home
- Expenses of entering into or breaking a lease
- Home improvements to help sell home
- Loss on sale home
- Loss from disposing of membership in clubs
- Mortgage penalties
- Pre-move house hunting expenses
- Real Estate taxes

- Refitting of carpet and draperies
- Return trips to former home
- Security deposits
- Storage charges except those incurred in transit and for foreign moves

So taxpayers that meet all of the above requirements want to keep their receipts related to the move. They can provide backup for some real tax savings.

For more information about the moving expense deduction, read IRS Publication 521 and IRS Topic 455 on the IRS.gov website.

Chapter 9 Retirement Account Deduction

The IRS wants people to save for their retirement. As a result, they offer some tax benefits. There are many types of retirement accounts but all have the goal of helping individuals save for retirement in a tax advantaged way.

Here is a quick list of the different types of retirement accounts:

- Traditional IRA
- ROTH IRA
- SEP
- SIMPLE
- 401k
- 403B
- 457 Plans
- Profit Sharing
- Defined Benefit
- Governmental Plans
- Money Purchase Plans

First we'll go over Traditional IRAs. These retirement accounts allow individuals to contribute up to $5,500 per year in contributions that help them lower their taxable income. $6,500 for anyone age 50 or older. That's the main tax advantage. Lowering the tax bill for the year.

Below is what the annual summary of contributions looks like for this account. That amount is what goes on the tax return.

☒ CORRECTED (if checked)			
TRUSTEE'S or ISSUER'S name, street address, city or town, state or province, country, and ZIP or foreign postal code **XYZ Financial**	**1** IRA contributions (other than amounts in boxes 2-4, 8-10, 13a, and 14a) $	OMB No. 1545-0747 20**14** Form **5498**	**IRA Contribution Information**
	2 Rollover contributions $ 0		
	3 Roth IRA conversion amount $	**4** Recharacterized contributions $	**Copy B**
TRUSTEE'S or ISSUER'S federal identification no. **11-1231231**	PARTICIPANT'S social security number **123-45-6789**	**5** Fair market value of account $50000.00	**6** Life insurance cost included in box 1 $	**For Participant**
PARTICIPANT'S name **Susan Walters**	**7** IRA ☒ SEP ☐ SIMPLE ☐ Roth IRA ☐ **8** SEP contributions $	**9** SIMPLE contributions $	This information is being furnished to the Internal Revenue Service.
Street address (including apt. no.) **1111 A Street**	**10** Roth IRA contributions $	**11** If checked, required minimum distribution for 2015 ☐	
	12a RMD date	**12b** RMD amount $	
City or town, state or province, country, and ZIP or foreign postal code **St.Cloud, MN 56303**	**13a** Postponed contribution $	**13b** Year **13c** Code	
	14a Repayments $	**14b** Code	
Account number (see instructions) **555T**	**15a** FMV of certain specified assets $	**15b** Code(s)	

Form **5498** (keep for your records) www.irs.gov/form5498 Department of the Treasury - Internal Revenue Service

The IRS does have a phase on who can contribute to an IRA and get the deduction and how much they make. Basically the more money a person makes, the less likely they are going to be able to take the traditional IRA contribution deduction. The table below goes through their guidelines:

If Your Filing Status Is...	And Your Modified AGI Is...	Then You Can Take...
single or **head of household**	$61,000 or less	a full deduction up to the amount of your <u>contribution limit</u>.
	more than $61,000 but less than $71,000	a partial deduction.

If Your Filing Status Is...	And Your Modified AGI Is...	Then You Can Take...
	$71,000 or more	no deduction.
married filing jointly or **qualifying widow(er)**	$98,000 or less	a full deduction up to the amount of your <u>contribution limit</u>.
	more than $98,000 but less than $118,000	a partial deduction.
	$118,000 or more	no deduction.
married filing separately	less than $10,000	a partial deduction.
	$10,000 or more	no deduction.
If you file separately and did not live with your spouse at any time during the year, your IRA deduction is determined under the "single" filing status.		

Next there are Roth IRAs. Now the contributions to Roths every year don't offer a benefit on a tax return. However, when a person starts to take distributions from the Roth IRA they won't have to pay taxes on the money they take out.

The remainder of the tax advantaged retirement accounts go through a taxpayer's job or their own self-employment.

Here they are:

- SEP
- SIMPLE
- 401k
- 403B
- 457 Plans
- Profit Sharing
- Defined Benefit
- Governmental Plans
- Money Purchase Plans

With each one of these accounts the most important part is to get the amount that was contributed to the account from the year end statement. That way it can be put it on their taxes.

So taxpayers looking for a great way to save for the future and get a tax benefit should look long and hard at retirement accounts. The IRS offers some really incentives in contributing to them.

For more information about retirement account deductions, read IRS publication 590-A on the IRS.gov website.

Chapter 10 Earned Income Tax Credit

According to the IRS, every year, 1 in 5 workers overlooks taking advantage of the earned income tax. Don't be one of those people if you qualify.

Here's how the IRS describes the Earned Income Tax Credit:

"The Earned Income Tax Credit, EITC or EIC, is a benefit for working people with low to moderate income. To qualify, you must meet certain requirements and file a tax return, even if you do not owe any tax or are not required to file. EITC reduces the amount of tax you owe and may give you a refund."

So, of course, the first question is, how does someone qualify for the earned income tax credit? Well, the IRS has done a good job of spelling that out. This chart below shows the max income you can make to qualify. If your adjustable gross income is less than the amount in your category, then you can take the credit.

If filing...	Qualifying Children Claimed			
	Zero	**One**	**Two**	**Three or more**
Single, Head of Household or Widowed	$14,880	$39,296	$44,648	$47,955
Married Filing Jointly	$20,430	$44,846	$50,198	$53,505

Investment income has to be less than $3,400.

So once a taxpayer finds out they qualify for the EITC they need to keep in mind what the maximum available benefit is for them. Here's the guidance the IRS provides:

What are the Maximum Credit Amounts Available for the Earned Income Credit?

The maximum amount of credit for Tax Year 2016 is:

$6,269 with three or more qualifying children

$5,572 with two qualifying children

$3,373 with one qualifying child

$506 with no qualifying children

So individuals that meet these requirements want to make sure they get all of their information together to take this credit. It can make a world of difference when it comes to getting a bigger refund.

For more information about the earned income credit, read IRS publication 596 on the IRS.gov website.

Chapter 11   Educator Expenses

Every year Tax Assurances prepares tax returns for a number of people in the education profession. They all spend countless hours preparing to help educate young children. Along with that time, these educators spend their own money to helping educate children. The IRS rewards that effort in a small way by providing a tax benefit.

As a result, the IRS allows teachers, instructors, counselors, principals, and aides that work at least 900 hours in elementary or secondary schools deductions of up to $250 of any unreimbursed expenses.

Those expenses include:

- books
- supplies
- computer equipment
- Other equipment that they use in the classroom.

The IRS does have these following requirements on taking these expenses as a deduction:

"Qualified expenses are deductible only to the extent a number of such expenses exceed the following amounts for the tax year:

- *The interest on qualified U.S. savings bonds that you excluded from income because you paid qualified higher education expenses,*

- *Any distribution from a qualified tuition program that you excluded from income,*

- *Any tax-free withdrawals from your Coverdell education savings accounts,*

- *Any reimbursed expenses not reported to you in box 1 of your Form W-2 (PDF)."*

For more information about the educator expense deduction, read IRS Topic 458 on the IRS.gov website.

Chapter 12   Child & Dependent Care Credit

Families are working harder and longer every day. We also live in a time where both individuals in a household have to work. As a result, other family members are left in the care of other people. And with constrained family budgets the IRS wanted to step in and help.

As a result, they provide a tax benefit for the cost of care for family members. There are criteria in order to qualify for the benefit and here is how the IRS outlines that:

1. *The care must have been provided for one or more qualifying persons. A qualifying person is your dependent child age 12 or younger when the care was provided. Additionally, your spouse and certain other individuals who are physically or mentally incapable of self-care may also be qualifying persons. You must identify each qualifying person on your tax return.*

2. *The care must have been provided so you – and your spouse if you are married filing jointly – could work or look for work.*

3. *You – and your spouse if you file jointly – must have earned income from wages, salaries, and tips, other taxable employee compensation or net earnings from self-employment. One spouse may be considered as having earned income if they were a full-time student or were physically or mentally unable to care for themselves.*

4. *The payments for care cannot be paid to your spouse, to the parent of your qualifying person, to someone you can claim as your dependent on your return, or to your child who will not be age 19 or older by the end of*

the year even if he or she is not your dependent. You must identify the care provider(s) on your tax return.

5. *Your filing status must be single, married filing jointly, head of household or qualifying widow(er) with a dependent child.*

6. *The qualifying person must have lived with you for more than half of the year. There are exceptions for the birth or death of a qualifying person, or a child of divorced or separated parents. See Publication 503, Child and Dependent Care Expenses.*

7. *The credit can be up to 35 percent of your qualifying expenses, depending upon your adjusted gross income.*

8. *For the year, you may use up to $3,000 of expenses paid in a year for one qualifying individual or $6,000 for two or more qualifying individuals to figure the credit.*

9. *The qualifying expenses must be reduced by the amount of any dependent care benefits provided by your employer that you deduct or exclude from your income.*

10. *If you pay someone to come to your home and care for your dependent or spouse, you may be a household employer and may have to withhold and pay social security and Medicare tax and pay federal unemployment tax. See Publication 926, Household Employer's Tax Guide.*

Here's the IRS form that captures the total costs to the parents on the tax return. Again the software should fill this in.

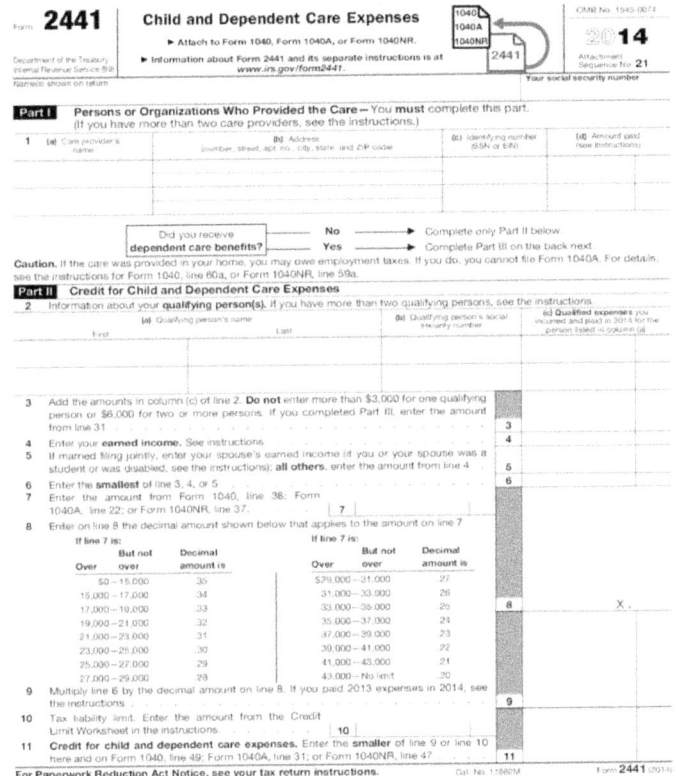

So taxpayers that have their children in daycare every day want to keep a record of how much they spend. At the end of the year it can have some real tax benefits.

For more information about the child and dependent care credits, read IRS Publication 503 on the IRS.gov website.

Conclusion

We understand that the tax code can be confusing and difficult to read through. That's why it's our sincere hope that this book gives readers clarity and tax benefits they can use.

We hope that all of our client experiences came through in this book. Again, we've met with tax clients for years going over their circumstance and looking for as many tax benefits as possible for them.